psalms of a black mother

By
Theresa Greenwood

The Warner Press
Anderson, Indiana

©1970, Warner Press, Inc.

All Rights Reserved

Library of Congress Catalog Card No. 72-127138

ISBN 0 87162 110 X

Printed in the United States of America

To Charles, Lisa, and Marc,
and my parents:
Hubert and Lillian Winfrey.
And to those mothers everywhere
who believe only God
can heal our troubled world.

Illustrations for this book
were arranged by John Silvey.
Drawings were supplied by:
Coleman Hill
Hartwell Nance
Jack Parnell
Fred Reel
John Silvey
Cover design by Jack Parnell.

PREFACE

Psalms of a Black Mother reflects the black mother's relationship to God. She trusts and talks to him about the little and most mundane affairs of her life.

These psalms tell of her ups and downs: hopes, disappointments; joys, fears; triumphs, failures.

This tribute echos the saga of that courageous black mother who stood by her family though often deserted by mate, friends, institutions, and even a nation.

She has been accused of dominating her domain, making what sociologists call a "matriarchal home." But tribute is due her, for she stood by her family during the storms of the ages. She gave them love, affection, and guidance, the glue that holds the family together.

Slavery taught her to take the lead and heal the wounds of its system. She made the most of life when her men and boys were stolen from her. But her faith and hope strengthened the family and provided the incubator for the newborn movement for liberation, pride, self-respect, and creative aspirations of the black man today.

Constantly living without the "frills" of life, she found a far richer gift from God.

PROLOGUE

They once saw the innocent smile of a slave
and assumed I was content with my lot
the chains that once made me moan
opened my soul to sing of freedom.

A sound drifted across the plantations and fields
and found its way into my heart as a song
a song with a melody that touched a nerve
then spread its mournful tune all over the world.

Even though my voice was soft and gentle
lately I've had to talk louder for people to hear
Many paused to bend their ears
but few have listened.

As I turn to find my new place for the long hard
day ahead I smell the venom of ghettos that
  profit the landlords.
People tell me to wake up and live
And now that I'm awake
I find nothing but the sleep of death.

I know now that just as a mighty river's course
cannot be changed with the dropping of a single stone
Neither can a world of injustice and inequity
be wiped clean with a flood of saccharin sentiment.

*I watch daisys grow everywhere now
in fields
pots
and gardens
They symbolize truth and love
for the restless world
But when their petals
are streaked with age
and decay
does man's faith also wrinkle
and turn brown
falling to a hard winter earth?
Or do the seeds of its tomorrow
like words of Your promise
filter softly down
on moist, waiting soil
to rest and blossom
in a springtime of eternity?*

*I don't know if I can hem this dress one
    more time
The punctured holes along the hem are mingling
and Mary's going to feel bad
But she's gotta wear it just one more time
then maybe I can get her a "new" one at the
    rummage sale
We're gonna make it fine
I can feel it in my bones
The Lord provides for those that wait
and trust Him, even for their littlest needs.*

O Lord
this gray iceberg of bitterness
that hides inside
is cold and harsh
It shuns the warm glow of Your love
and pushes on the back door of my mind
Others see only the frigid top as it juts up
but the swollen basement part
keeps me off balance
It pulls me under
yanking
tugging
splitting
But the custodian of my mind
admonishes me to look up
and melt
warm over
the leftovers of my bitterness
It beckons me to
cast overboard the zeros of life
and reach
aspire
hope
live for the fulfillment of Your promises.

*They think my children can't learn
or don't want to learn
Sometimes they even talk down to them—
insult their intelligence—
and make them feel they're not worth much
Then when its time to go to college
they ask, "What's the matter, BOY,
don't you know anything?"
They even told them all they'd ever need
   to know
was how to sign their names on
checks
bills
traffic tickets
and bail slips
Sometimes they didn't mark him untamed
but in their unharried
uncaring
uncompromising gestures
they made ugly words
unnecessary.*

Yesterday
my little boy got lost
in the big store downtown
It wasn't long
before a nice man came
smiling
to show me where to find him
Life is that way
Once I was lost
and You came
smiled
took my hand
and showed me the Way.

Look at me,
tired
and not pretty enough to greet my husband
curlers in my hair
and my face pasty, lathery with creams
It's only five minutes and he'll be home
Maybe he'll be just a little late
then I can
comb a special flip
throw on a pretty dress
pick up the toys
Just an extra minute
would do wonders.

Often I sit and amuse myself
with uncommon thoughts
like how far man has come
All the way from the witch doctor to the
    heart surgeon
from the mud hut to skyscrapers
from the cave to the moon!
And then I wonder, how far have we come
in learning to live together
be forgiving
healing
comforting
loving and
praising Your name?

Father,
sometimes I don't know where to turn
As I set this table I feel left out
without hope
without direction
I hear people refer to me
"You people"
"They"
"Them"
But they never stop
to look and see just me
Me with my smooth velvety black skin
my wide nose and heavy lips
Me, Lord,
Your child too.
I plead for them to see just one
pick me out from the masses

*and judge me on what I am
Maybe I can sing a soulful song
or cook a mess of greens, better'n the next fellow
But whatever
I'm me and that's all I want them to see
Me, a person of dignity
with skin maybe as dark as cinnamon
or terribly tan
But as rich as ever
because I am one of Your precious children.
Give them eyes to see me
one person
one woman with
ambitions
weaknesses, struggles
and most of all
feelings.*

*My Willie rushed in the other night
huffing, panting
nervous and jittery
throwing and slinging in his dad's closet
He was ready for trouble
I could see it on his face
I could feel the filthy breath of hate
He was seething, ready to go get even
But Lord, You stepped in
and now Willie's asleep
   behind that door over there
Maybe tomorrow
   things ain't gonna look so bad to Willie.*

I'm a working mama and I wish it weren't so
I need to be home tending my kids
washing
ironing
scraping, cleaning
and doing something special to make my
house a home
But I gotta work....
I feel guilty leaving my house looking so bad
ironing stacked on the bed
and the dishes in the sink
But here I am waiting for the bus to take me
out in the pale coolness of the suburbs so
I can wash
iron
scrape, clean
and make "their" house a home.

Sometimes my mind is a slum
cluttered
dark and musty
Blow some clean air here
dig
plow away the debris
Raze the ugliness of hate
Bring spring with its new life
and let the hope of love move in.
Redevelop and urbanize my vain labels
Let me even love those that built my world
and those that collect its plunder.
Those garbage cans reeking in the alley
once symbolized my life
but now I escape its squalor
I'm made anew by Your grace.

*I'm just like any other mama
I have fears, joys, burdens
I too weep when
the war takes my son
and buries his future in
uncertainty
dank piles of misery.
I cannot help but feel
despair
lost
without peace
deprived
without consolation
But now I've put my trust in You
my only hope.
And from my sole to my crown
I feel the warmth of
assurance
peace
and eternal hope.*

My son's a scientist,
a bright searching young man
He's got three degrees
but no salvation
He's got honors
but no honor
He's got charity
but no love
He's got "things"
but really nothing
The test tube is his church
and carbolic acid his revelation
Lord,
Open the eyes of my boy who's
been blinded by a
thimbleful of
knowledge.

*Sometimes
I feel old
useless
and ugly
I reach and nothing comes
I speak and no one hears
I sing and no heart is moved
But then I pray
and Lord
You listen.*

*Sometimes,
I feel I'm talking to a dead world
A world of people with bodies
but no hearts
They hear my children cry
but shut their ears
They see my crumbling walls
but turn away
Many feel my endless pain
but soon numb their skins
They say I'm unfit
untouchable
But Lord, You, greater than any man,
came to this shack
sat in that raggedy old chair*

ate stale bread with me
The place was a mess
I hadn't even felt like sweeping
and it was cold and dark
But You said You'd take me as I am
Just as I am!
When You stopped to visit that day
You touched my empty heart
healed my broken dreams
Now beauty floods my soul.
I will listen when they cry,
build when their walls crumble
and heal their pain
with Your unbent
love.

We live in a tarnished, gilded world
where my son's more concerned with his
thick bushy Afro
black power
clenched fist
the protocol of equality
the latest militant handshake
or the next demonstration march
He takes to the soapbox
for everything but for You.
I'm concerned, dear Lord.
In fact, I'm worried.
I have no place to turn but to You
Have I failed to plant the seed of
hope
peace won
not through tall flimsy signs
nor big shiny lapel buttons
but rather
in the blood of Your salvation?

I'm a mean mama
While others play
dally away the hours
I call my children to
pray
I admonish them to talk
with You
at school
work
and even during the ball game
Yes, I suppose I am a mean mama
but one day
my children will say, M-E-A-N
is another way to spell
LOVE.

*Once I thought blessings came from a
    heavenly automat
where you deposited "goodness" coins and
then little doors opened and blessings would
    pour out
But now I know that God's blessings and love
are not for sale
not that complicated
He gives them to us for free!
When you faithfully open your heart to Him
doors, big doors, will open
and pour out blessings
blessings too great to number
too BIG to be contained
in little compartments of the world's automats.*

*The constant rhythm of this new music
scours my thoughts
teases my wisdom
I see youngsters jerking
moving senseless to its beats
heedless of what it all means
The swirling colors that dance on the walls
are twisted, grotesque
and distorted
How long I've listened
wondering where it all will end
But now I realize
just as the tone of the artist,
the architect, the fashion designer
has a stroke of the primitive's brush
so has man's morals, creative expressions
his thoughts and too
his music.*

Someone called my little girl "nigger" yesterday
Lord, I knew it was coming sooner or later
But it didn't really hurt her
   like they'd intended
'cause we'd talked before
Sure, she's black
but she's proud too
It took three hundred years for people
   to love being black—
a long time to undo the hurt

*Today when I was making Sloppy Joes
my little girl's new friend was a face
   I'd never seen
Guess who joined us for supper tonight?
It was then I thought
If only we adults could be like children
forgiving
loving
forgetting
and living as You commanded
Thank You for the wisdom of a child.*

*Sometimes, I felt the sun
    didn't even shine on my street
I thought it was just for the rich
the safe,
    the other guy
And by the time it came my way
the warmth had gone away
But I found a sun
that shines even when the sky is hazy
and storm clouds roll into place
The everlasting love of Jesus
never fades
    eclipses
    or hides
It shines on all sides of my midnight world.*

*I don't hear much mention
about Your coming again
People seem to talk about everything else
things like
diets
bank accounts
new cars
fancy boats and yachts
Quietly, Your word pleads us to await that day
yet we seal our ears
A long time ago, the world buzzed
with the same silly chatter
Yet only one man listened
—and built a boat.*

*Touch my twisted
abandoned mind
heal it
mold
sanctify
cleanse
settle the dust of uncertainty
seal the cracks
solder the broken lines of communication
splice
tranquilize
awaken
amputate the evil that lurks inside.*

*Obsidian faces
reflecting militant thoughts
rough black hands
close-cropped woolly hair
pawned minds willed to unfamiliar hands
Forging
strangling
wrestling
revolting
finding inequity in
the geometry of life.*

*Where are the days I used to know
when time moved slowly
and children took a year to grow an inch?
Why must I live in a world where I rush
to eat
to sleep
to pray?*

When the death angels
   took my Roy last night
I didn't have anything left to live for
I pulled the shades of life
and locked the doors
then waited
When Roy died, my faith died too
He took it with him
and then I was here with nothing
Where had I lost hold?
Roy was strong and believed
I thought I did too
but I had borrowed a faith
and when he left
so did my faith
Now—without Roy to lean on
but
with Your hand to guide,
maybe I can find the way
alone.

Once,
I tried to buy salvation
with saving stamps
coupons
warranties
stocks and bonds
Now I know it's free
free to breathe
to feel
to live
This new life
is so fragrant
fresh as spring showers
as new as tomorrow
yet as ancient as
Your
Word.

*They say the age of Aquarius is here
but listening to the LPs of my memory
I heard another generation echo similar chants
Still here and without change is the
starving child,
the man without ears,
the ebony slave
pushing
marching
demonstrating
singing with voices of black velvet
and pleading
for a chance to be himself.*

*There's something sweet
innocent
trusting
irresistible
restful
and eternal about the smile
of a child.
The fate of the world is stormy
yet a child's smile can
heal the woes of
races
neighbors
nations
and man's search for
himself.*

Steam gushing
collecting in droplets about my head
pots simmering
pressure cooker clicking
I get tired
standing here in the kitchen all day
roasting
baking
frying
blending
folding
day after day
If it wasn't for You I'd have
pots sticking
roasts sizzling
baking bronzing
frying frizzling
Everything would be all
purple panic.

*One day, Lord, You knocked
so gently
I scarcely heard
You reached out
I shut my eyes
then
You touched my heart
I felt the compelling tug
of compassion
of charity
bidding me
to open my rusty door
step out into the sunlight
and follow You.*

Spring came to my heart yesterday
Tender blossoms of love
sprouted
peeked out of my winter heart
The roaring winds stopped blowing
and let the warmth of God's love
envelop
jolt a silent soul.
I felt good
For the joy of the summer it promises
is the hope of
Your kingdom to come.

*The army's done took my Jim
took him away to fight some people
on the other side of the world
He's so young, Lord,
He ain't ready for a man's job.
I taught him Your commandment, "Do not kill"
now I don't know what to do
He had to go
ain't nothing I can do about it
Take care of him
I beg You, Lord.*

Once

someone called me a little lighthouse
flashing its guiding ray
to those who pass by
Now they don't need me anymore
They've got computers to do the job
I'd just be in the way
But one day I realized
the littlest lighthouse
can brighten the way better
past the smaller stones of life.

The mailman ain't brought my check yet
It's been almost a week and
I don't know where to turn
I can't go down there and demand my money
They'll just say that "thinking machine"
*   broke down*
How can a computer feel my pains?
Well, maybe it can think and remember
but the most important part is missing—
it's got no heart.

*My soul was parched in the desert of anger
It seemed right to let the burning bitterness
take over
I had the right, didn't I?
I had been hurt
wronged
used
enslaved
But one day I came to an oasis
of cool life-giving water that
put out fires of hate
quenched revenge
and filled my soul with
the power
of forgiveness.*

*My children, they are good kids
but I can't give them everything they need
That school is a wise place
but I just ain't got the money
every time they need it
If it ain't a pack of paper
it's a new box of crayons
I can't seem to make ends meet
and with the baby coming and all
I got my hands right full
Lord, sometimes I'm
a nylon soul
easily run
worn thin with time
sometimes sheer
sometimes opaque.*

*The knots of men that gather on the corners
spit and curse
and forget that You live
They take my son's mind and teach him how
to take the easy way out
They beckon my daughters to stray.
O Lord, untie those knots and
bind them with Your grace,
The dull sage that rots their hopes
please sweeten with real love
Rinse away the saccharin happiness
so that one day these tired, lazy men
can find their places
with their forgotten families.*

Yesterday, Lord, my son came home
He's been gone so long
been to school and away working
his papa would've been so proud
now he's home to visit mama
Today he took a walk—
the town's changed so much
Just when he was about to cross the street
someone yelled, "Hey, nigger,
what's your name?"
Softly he answered, "Charles H. Wilson, III."
"You mean Charlie, don't you
All niggers are Charlies!"
Then he laughed and went his way
But my son the doctor wept a tear
a tear of compassion, pity
and looked upward toward the
God that loves my son and
the man he met on the street.

Last week the angels took my baby
He was so young
hadn't hardly been born yet
eyes still shut from this ugly old world
But Lord, You saw fit that he not stay here
in this place
My heart is empty
Sometimes it's so hard to still have faith
pitifully hard
But with Your hand of mercy
I can live
love
and give bread to another's
starving child.

Inside I am crying,
  but my face is silent
Inside I shout loudly,
  but my tongue is still
This is terrible, I feel down
But I know that You can reach down
and pick me out of this dross
A big mama like me
sitting here so low
I must wipe my eyes
before the children see the stain
the tears have left.

*Sometimes my mind is a deep dark cave
black with musty cobwebs
hanging there from the yesterdays
Chink a hole in the other end
and let the
Good News blow through.*

*Today, Lord,
I feel free
full of love for everyone
But stand by with Your power
When I may stray
be there to pull me back
into the game again.*

Where, O Lord
must I go?
I am tired
I need rest
Breathe fresh tranquility
on this poor soul.

Lord,
You made the world so perfect
and all we had to do was obey
But somehow we got a big hang-up
and tried to run it our way
Look what we've done to Your nice world:
littered the air with acid
and peppered the waters with filth
Where did our conscience go?
Who did we think we were?

*Last night we popped some corn
the kids and I
There's still a grain or two
I forgot to get with the broom
But, oh, those faces, I'll always remember:
smiling
laughing
giggling
imagining those kernels to be
snowflakes
roaring lions
gentle lambs
puppets, people
and all sorts of things
Lord, Your majesty and mystery
are everywhere
even in a kernel of corn.*

I know it was only yesterday
  I bought these stockings
but they're full of runs now
I can't go meet Annabelle's teacher looking
  like this
She'll be so 'shamed of me
I tried to keep them good
washed them in that "mild stuff"
wrapped them in a towel
and hung them up carefully
But that nervous cat down the hall
grabbed at me before I could say, scat!
What am I gonna do?

*Earthquakes everywhere
in the cities
schools
minds of youth
Thunder rolls
Governments shake
I keep my hand in Yours
and in the midst of all
I live on steady ground
—or in calm seas
with peaceful thoughts.*

Winter:
Heavy black caldrons of beans
flavored with ham hocks
cornbread
steaming mugs of sassafras.

Then Spring:
Grandma with her
sulphur and molasses
   to thin my blood
I remember
Mama
Granny
they took good care of me.

*My mind's camera
can't focus long range or
spit out prints in seconds
But it presses images
moods
feelings
in the pages of my memory
Imprints that will
never fade
grow brittle
in that album I take to my grave.*

Here I sit in my infested cubicle
with wall to wall roaches
the rhythm of dripping water
is my only music
Shattered
cracked plaster
dictates where I hang pictures
and the taped window panes
peeling paint
missing panes
are but outward symbols of
my inner ghetto.

*Thank You
Dear Lord
for the quiet people garden
where I can go to pray
Where red
black
yellow
brown
and white
together
all love to please You
by loving each other.*

*Lord, its morning in the world of love
and the day has just begun
I've got baskets of charity to unpack
I've heard that here morning never ends
the sun shines bright and days go on
one after another, like a forever Spring
In this world, my basket will never
grow empty.*

*I found it takes more than
a beautiful color
to get into Your kingdom
It takes more than vaults of money
or charitable deeds to folks like me
You gotta build mountains of believing
unleash oceans of good thoughts
shape worlds of real brotherhood.*

*The young people are saying "Turn on"
"Do your thing"
and "Let it all hang out"
I don't understand all they say
but I say to them
Tune in
Listen
Heed
and "Hang in there" with Christ.*

Here I am again in front of the TV
it's time for my stories
Sometimes I feel so sad watching those folks
and all their troubles
I could cry out . . .
But I guess they do me some good
They make me realize how wonderful
things really are for me.

   I don't have to take a back seat in
   the bus of Your kingdom
   or reside at the rear end
      of Your world
   I can stand with pride up front
      with others
   cause You're the conductor.

*Here it's Saturday
and I promised Mr. Gunyon
I'd pay my bill
He's let me run up my credit
and still I can't pay
Last month it was the same thing
but he let me have a little more time
Things cost so much these days
and my welfare check
   ain't no rubber band
Seems like just when I get
   an extra penny ahead
something always comes up
something I didn't know about at all
You said You'd care for even the sparrows
and deep down inside, I know
You will provide for me.*

Sometimes I feel You have left me here, Lord,
to bear this burden all alone
There's not even a whisper of Your presence
so I sink in my chair and stare out at the night
a night so black, so bleak
I can hear only the crunching of snow
pressing under the feet of the hurried
The room is dark and the children are asleep
I know You're here with me
but I feel so alone
No bread for tomorrow, the beans all gone
Neal's socks, nothing but holes
and Lilly's dress won't last another day
O Lord, I know You care
I know You hear, but all is loneliness
I think back on the child I once held to my bosom
as his life leaked away
It would've been another mouth to feed
I guess I really don't understand at all
Things could be worse
But for some reason I can't see that far tonight
Now, everything is all darkness
ebony
hopeless.

Lord
it ain't easy being a mama
Sometimes I wonder if I'll ever get the hang of it
Day after day goes by and
I find none of them like today
It's OJT* all the way.
Sometimes I want to throw my hands up
  in despair
but when I look up to You
I find hope
I find that inner peace that cools my sweaty face
that helps me find joy even in
the hot dishwater, wrinkling and aging my hands
the constant churn of grime
watering neglected plants
feeding the dog
and remembering to crack the windows
  in the kids' room at night.
O Lord, I know it's You that sustains and keeps me
I couldn't do it all alone
For little things I praise You
For those things too big to tote I praise You
Thank You, Lord.

*On the Job Training

EPILOGUE

*Long ago I believed
   that being a black mama was
having kinky hair
heavy lips
swaying to the rhythm of her soul
wearing a red bandanna if she chose
loving blackeyed peas and candied sweets
working hard
having high ambitions for her children
longing to be really free
struggling to unglue the stamp of slavery
a Simba, wrestling with her identity
having pride
being an apostle of God's love
aspiring
hoping
and never giving up. . .
And now I know
IT IS!*